JCL & VSAM

Programming Guide

First Edition

Venkatesh Ramasamy

Lulu Press, Inc.
3101 Hillsborough Street
Raleigh, North Carolina, 27607
United States of America

JCL & VSAM Programming Guide, First Edition

by Venkatesh Ramasamy

International Standard Book Number (ISBN): 978-1-79486-775-8

Printed in the United States of America.

First Edition published on January 2020.

Disclaimer

No patent liability is assumed with respect to the use of the information contained herein. Although every precaution has been taken in the preparation of this book, the publisher and author assume no responsibility for errors or omissions. No liability is assumed for incidental or consequential damage in connection with or arising out of the use of the information or programs contained herein.

Printed and bounded in Lulu Press, Inc., 3101 Hillsborough Street, Raleigh, North Carolina, 27607, United States of America.

Preface

Job Control Language (or JCL) specifies how programs are executed on the mainframe. JCL functions are the interface between the programs and the operating system. Since JCL has the ability to define data set names, parameters and system output devices, the individual programs can be flexible in their use because these items are not hard coded in the programs. Without the need for re-compiling, the same program may be used to access different data sets and behave differently based on parameters specified in the JCL. VSAM is a file system used in IBM's MVS, OS/390 and ZOS operating systems. It offers standard sequential files, keyed or indexed files, and files whose records are retrieved by number, as well as other types used primarily by database management systems and its datasets are defined using JCL statements. JCL & VSAM can be difficult because of the way they are used. A normal programming language, however difficult, soon becomes familiar through constant usage. This contrasts with JCL & VSAM in which language features are used infrequently that one never becomes familiar.

The book "JCL & VSAM Programming Guide" attempts to provide simple explanation for beginners about various JCL & VSAM Programming concepts. This book is a single source you would need to quickly race up to speed and significantly enhance your skill and knowledge in JCL & VSAM. This has been designed as a self-study material for both beginners and experienced programmers. This book is organized with practical examples that will show you how to develop your program in JCL & VSAM. This book a perfect fit for all groups of people from beginners with no previous programming experience to programmers who already know JCL & VSAM and are ambitious to improve their style and reliability. Whether coding in JCL & VSAM is your hobby or your career, this book will enlighten you on your goal.

Happy Reading !!

About Programming Guide Series:

The titles in this programming guide series deals with technical descriptions of important software programming languages to give insights on how programming works and what it can be used for. These are ideal first books for beginners from a wide range of backgrounds like enterprise developer, technical manager, solution architect, tester, etc. This is an ideal place to begin mastering a new programming area and lay a solid foundation for further study. The curriculum of these books is carefully designed to reflect the needs of a diverse population, so there is something for everyone. The books in this programming guide series cover a broad range of topics including ANSI C, HTML, CSS, JavaScript, VBScript, JCL, VSAM, etc.

Warm Regards,
Venkatesh Ramasamy
twitter @rvenkateshbe

Author

Venkatesh Ramasamy is a senior quality engineer and technology consultant for a leading multinational company in Information Technology sector. He has excellent experience in managing enterprise IT project life cycle and has developed many software products for providing end-to-end IT services with optimized cost and improved quality. He is also vastly experienced in working with large insurers and financial services organizations based out of UK & US, for setting up independent test centers for their enterprise level quality engineering needs. He has very much interested in programming languages & web design technologies and has helped in developing wide variety of software products for the customers to successfully implement their new age corporate IT strategies.

Over the years he has presented and published many whitepapers at both national and international conferences and has also authored various technical articles in international magazines. He is also the author of several other programming books including ANSI C Programming Guide, HTML & CSS Programming Guide, JavaScript Programming Guide, JCL & VSAM Programming Guide and Handbook on 1000 Software Testing Tools.

You can reach him at his Twitter handle @rvenkateshbe.

Contents

Part: I - JCL & VSAM Programming

Part: II - JCL & VSAM Reference   36

JCL & VSAM

Programming Guide

PART - I

Programming Examples

01. Program to copy from one PS to another PS using IEBGENER

```
000100 //TCHN267#      JOB   ABC,NOTIFY=&SYSUID

000200 //STEP1         EXEC  PGM=IEBGENER

000300 //SYSPRINT      DD    SYSOUT=*

000400 //SYSUT1        DD    DSN=TCHN267.A.B,DISP=SHR

000500 //SYSUT2        DD    DSN=TCHN267.C.D,DISP=SHR

000600 //SYSIN         DD    DUMMY
```

02. Program to copy from one PS to another PDS member using IEBGENER

```
000100 //TCHN267#      JOB   ABC,NOTIFY=&SYSUID

000200 //STEP1         EXEC  PGM=IEBGENER

000300 //SYSPRINT      DD    SYSOUT=*

000400 //SYSUT1        DD    DSN=TCHN267.A.B,DISP=SHR

000500 //SYSUT2        DD
          DSN=TCHN267.VENKYTSO.PDS4(MEM1),DISP=SHR

000600 //SYSIN         DD    DUMMY
```

03. Program to copy from one PDS member to another PDS member using IEBGENER

```
000100 //TCHN267#      JOB   ABC,NOTIFY=&SYSUID

000200 //STEP1         EXEC  PGM=IEBGENER

000300 //SYSPRINT      DD    SYSOUT=*

000400 //SYSUT1        DD
          DSN=TCHN267.VENKYTSO.PDS4(MEM1),DISP=SHR

000500 //SYSUT2        DD
          DSN=TCHN267.VENKYTSO.PDS4(MEM2),DISP=SHR

000600 //SYSIN         DD    DUMMY
```

04. Program to copy from one PDS member to another non existing PDS member using IEBGENER

```
000100 //TCHN267#      JOB   ABC,NOTIFY=&SYSUID

000200 //STEP1         EXEC  PGM=IEBGENER

000300 //SYSPRINT      DD    SYSOUT=*

000400 //SYSUT1        DD
        DSN=TCHN267.VENKYTSO.PDS4(MEM1),DISP=SHR

000500 //SYSUT2        DD
        DSN=TCHN267.VENKYTSO.PS4,DISP=(NEW,CATLG,DELETE),

000510 //
        SPACE=(TRK,(1,1),RLSE),DCB=(LRECL=80,BLKSIZE=800,RECFM=FB)

000600 //SYSIN         DD    DUMMY
```

05. Program to copy from one PDS to another PDS using IEBCOPY

```
000100 //TCHN267#      JOB   ABC,NOTIFY=&SYSUID

000200 //STEP1         EXEC  PGM=IEBCOPY

000300 //SYSPRINT      DD    SYSOUT=*

000400 //DD1           DD    DSN=TCHN267.VENKYTSO.PDS11,DISP=SHR

000500 //DD2           DD    DSN=TCHN267.VENKYTSO.PDS12,DISP=SHR

000600 //SYSIN         DD    *

000700                COPY INDD=DD1,OUTDD=DD2

000800 /*

000900 //
```

06. Program to copy from one PDS to another PDS by selecting required members using IEBCOPY

```
000100 //TCHN267#      JOB    ABC,NOTIFY=&SYSUID
000200 //STEP1         EXEC  PGM=IEBCOPY
000300 //SYSPRINT      DD    SYSOUT=*
000400 //DD1           DD    DSN=TCHN267.VENKYTSO.PDS11,DISP=SHR
000500 //DD2           DD    DSN=TCHN267.VENKYTSO.PDS12,DISP=SHR
000600 //SYSIN         DD    *
000700                 COPY INDD=DD1,OUTDD=DD2
000710                 SELECT MEMBER=(MEM1,MEM2,MEM3)
000800 /*
000900 //
```

07. Program to copy from one PDS to another PDS by excluding unrequired members using IEBCOPY

```
000100 //TCHN267#      JOB    ABC,NOTIFY=&SYSUID
000200 //STEP1         EXEC  PGM=IEBCOPY
000300 //SYSPRINT      DD    SYSOUT=*
000400 //DD1           DD    DSN=TCHN267.VENKYTSO.PDS11,DISP=SHR
000500 //DD2           DD    DSN=TCHN267.VENKYTSO.PDS12,DISP=SHR
000600 //SYSIN         DD    *
000700                 COPY INDD=DD1,OUTDD=DD2
000710                 EXCLUDE MEMBER=(MEM1,MEM3)
000720 /*
000730 //
```

08. Program to compress PDS using IEBCOPY

```
000100 //TCHN267#      JOB   ABC,NOTIFY=&SYSUID
000200 //STEP1         EXEC PGM=IEBCOPY
000300 //SYSPRINT      DD    SYSOUT=*
000400 //DD1           DD    DSN=TCHN267.VENKYTSO.PDS11,DISP=SHR
000600 //SYSIN         DD    *
000700                 COPY INDD=DD1,OUTDD=DD1
000720 /*
000730 //
```

09. Program to compare two PDS using IEBCOMPR

```
000100 //TCHN267#      JOB   ABC,NOTIFY=&SYSUID
000200 //STEP1         EXEC PGM=IEBCOMPR
000300 //SYSPRINT      DD    SYSOUT=*
000400 //SYSUT1        DD    DSN=TCHN267.VENKYTSO.PDS11,DISP=OLD
000500 //SYSUT2        DD    DSN=TCHN267.VENKYTSO.PDS12,DISP=OLD
000600 //SYSIN DD *
000700                 COMPARE TYPORG=PO
000800 /*
000900 //
```

10. Program to compare two PS using IEBCOMPR

```
000100 //TCHN267#      JOB   ABC,NOTIFY=&SYSUID
000200 //STEP1         EXEC  PGM=IEBCOMPR
000300 //SYSPRINT      DD    SYSOUT=*
```

```
000400 //SYSUT1        DD    DSN=TCHN267.VENKYTSO.PS6,DISP=OLD

000500 //SYSUT2        DD    DSN=TCHN267.VENKYTSO.PS7,DISP=OLD

000600 //SYSIN         DD    *

000700                 COMPARE TYPORG=PS

000800 /*

000900 //
```

11. Program to sort given PS in CH mode descending order and paste the sorted output to another PS using SORT

```
000100 //TCHN267#      JOB   ABC,NOTIFY=&SYSUID

000200 //STEP1         EXEC PGM=SORT

000300 //SYSOUT        DD    SYSOUT=*

000400 //SYSPRINT      DD    SYSOUT=*

000500 //SORTIN        DD    DSN=TCHN267.VENKYTSO.PS8,DISP=SHR

000600 //SORTOUT       DD    DSN=TCHN267.VENKYTSO.PS9,DISP=SHR

000700 //SORTWK01      DD    UNIT=SYSDA,SPACE=(CYL,(20,10),RLSE)

000800 //SYSIN         DD    *

000900                 SORT FIELDS=(1,3,CH,D)

001000 /*

001100 //
```

12. Program to sort given PS in CH mode ascending order and paste the sorted output to another PS using SORT

```
000100 //TCHN267#      JOB   ABC,NOTIFY=&SYSUID

000200 //STEP1         EXEC  PGM=SORT

000300 //SYSOUT        DD    SYSOUT=*
```

```
000400 //SYSPRINT     DD    SYSOUT=*

000500 //SORTIN       DD    DSN=TCHN267.VENKYTSO.PS8,DISP=SHR

000600 //SORTOUT      DD    DSN=TCHN267.VENKYTSO.PS9,DISP=SHR

000700 //SORTWK01     DD    UNIT=SYSDA,SPACE=(CYL,(20,10),RLSE)

000800 //SYSIN        DD    *

000900               SORT FIELDS=(1,3,CH,A)

001000 /*

001100 //
```

13. Program to sort given PS in AC mode descending order and paste the sorted output to another PS using SORT

```
000200 //TCHN267#     JOB   ABC,NOTIFY=&SYSUID

000300 //STEP1        EXEC  PGM=SORT

000400 //SYSOUT       DD    SYSOUT=*

000500 //SYSPRINT     DD    SYSOUT=*

000600 //SORTIN       DD    DSN=TCHN267.VENKYTSO.PS8,DISP=SHR

000700 //SORTOUT      DD    DSN=TCHN267.VENKYTSO.PS9,DISP=SHR

000800 //SORTWK01     DD    UNIT=SYSDA,SPACE=(CYL,(20,10),RLSE)

000900 //SYSIN        DD    *

001000               SORT FIELDS=(1,3,AC,D)

001100 /*

001200 //
```

14. Program to sort given PS in AC mode ascending order and paste the sorted output to another PS using SORT

```
000200 //TCHN267#      JOB   ABC,NOTIFY=&SYSUID
000300 //STEP1         EXEC  PGM=SORT
000400 //SYSOUT        DD    SYSOUT=*
000500 //SYSPRINT      DD    SYSOUT=*
000600 //SORTIN        DD    DSN=TCHN267.VENKYTSO.PS8,DISP=SHR
000700 //SORTOUT       DD    DSN=TCHN267.VENKYTSO.PS9,DISP=SHR
000800 //SORTWK01      DD    UNIT=SYSDA,SPACE=(CYL,(20,10),RLSE)
000900 //SYSIN         DD    *
001000                 SORT FIELDS=(1,3,AC,A)
001100 /*
001200 //
```

15. Program to sort given PS in AC mode descending order and paste the sorted output to another PS using SORT [without using SORTWK01]

```
000100 //TCHN267#      JOB   ABC,NOTIFY=&SYSUID
000200 //STEP1         EXEC  PGM=SORT
000300 //SYSOUT        DD    SYSOUT=*
000400 //SYSPRINT      DD    SYSOUT=*
000500 //SORTIN        DD    DSN=TCHN267.VENKYTSO.PS8,DISP=SHR
000600 //SORTOUT       DD    DSN=TCHN267.VENKYTSO.PS9,DISP=SHR
000700 //*SORTWK01     DD    UNIT=SYSDA,SPACE=(CYL,(20,10),RLSE)  {NO
NEED THIS}
000800 //SYSIN         DD    *
000900                 SORT FIELDS=(1,3,AC,D)
```

```
001000 /*

001100 //
```

16. Program to sort given PS in AC mode descending order and paste the sorted output to another PS without duplicating the records using SORT

```
000100 //TCHN267#      JOB   ABC,NOTIFY=&SYSUID

000200 //STEP1         EXEC  PGM=SORT

000300 //SYSOUT        DD    SYSOUT=*

000400 //SYSPRINT      DD    SYSOUT=*

000500 //SORTIN        DD     DSN=TCHN267.VENKYTSO.PS8,DISP=SHR

000600 //SORTOUT       DD     DSN=TCHN267.VENKYTSO.PS9,DISP=SHR

000700 //SORTWK01      DD     UNIT=SYSDA,SPACE=(CYL,(20,10),RLSE)

000800 //SYSIN         DD    *

000900                 SORT FIELDS=(1,3,AC,D)

000910                 SUM FIELDS=NONE

001000 /*

001100 //
```

17. Program to sort given PS in CH mode descending order and paste the sorted output to another PS with duplicating the records using SORT

```
000100 //TCHN267#      JOB   ABC,NOTIFY=&SYSUID

000200 //STEP1         EXEC  PGM=SORT

000300 //SYSOUT        DD    SYSOUT=*

000400 //SYSPRINT      DD    SYSOUT=*

000500 //SORTIN        DD    DSN=TCHN267.VENKYTSO.PS8,DISP=SHR

000600 //SORTOUT       DD    DSN=TCHN267.VENKYTSO.PS9,DISP=SHR
```

```
000700 //SORTWK01    DD    UNIT=SYSDA,SPACE=(CYL,(20,10),RLSE)

000800 //SYSIN       DD    *

000900              SORT FIELDS=(1,3,CH,D)

000910              SUM FIELDS=ALL

000920 /*

000930 //
```

18. Program to sort given PS in CH mode descending order and paste the sorted output to another PS and the duplicating records to another PS using SORT

```
000100 //TCHN267#    JOB   ABC,NOTIFY=&SYSUID

000200 //STEP1       EXEC  PGM=SORT

000300 //SYSOUT      DD    SYSOUT=*

000400 //SYSPRINT    DD    SYSOUT=*

000500 //SORTIN      DD    DSN=TCHN267.VENKYTSO.PS8,DISP=SHR

000600 //SORTOUT     DD    DSN=TCHN267.VENKYTSO.PS9,DISP=SHR

000610 //SORTXSUM    DD    DSN=TCHN267.VENKYTSO.PS10,DISP=SHR

000700 //SORTWK01    DD    UNIT=SYSDA,SPACE=(CYL,(20,10),RLSE)

000800 //SYSIN       DD    *

000900              SORT FIELDS=(1,3,CH,D)

000910              SUM FIELDS=NONE,XSUM

000920 /*

000930 //
```

19. Program to sort given PS in CH mode descending order and filter by particular word and then paste the sorted output to another PS using SORT

```
000100 //TCHN267#      JOB   ABC,NOTIFY=&SYSUID

000200 //STEP1         EXEC  PGM=SORT

000300 //SYSOUT        DD    SYSOUT=*

000400 //SYSPRINT      DD    SYSOUT=*

000500 //SORTIN        DD    DSN=TCHN267.VENKYTSO.PS11,DISP=SHR

000600 //SORTOUT       DD    DSN=TCHN267.VENKYTSO.PS9,DISP=SHR

000620 //SORTWK01      DD    UNIT=SYSDA,SPACE=(CYL,(20,10),RLSE)

000630 //SYSIN         DD    *

000640                 SORT FIELDS=COPY

000650                 INCLUDE COND=(20,10,CH,EQ,C'CHENNAI')

000660 /*

000670 //
```

20. Program to sort given PS in CH mode descending order and omit by particular word and then paste the sorted output to another PS using SORT

```
000100 //TCHN267#      JOB   ABC,NOTIFY=&SYSUID

000200 //STEP1         EXEC  PGM=SORT

000300 //SYSOUT        DD    SYSOUT=*

000400 //SYSPRINT      DD    SYSOUT=*

000500 //SORTIN        DD    DSN=TCHN267.VENKYTSO.PS11,DISP=SHR

000600 //SORTOUT       DD    DSN=TCHN267.VENKYTSO.PS9,DISP=SHR

000610 //SORTWK01      DD    UNIT=SYSDA,SPACE=(CYL,(20,10),RLSE)
```

```
000620 //SYSIN          DD    *

000630                  SORT FIELDS=COPY

000640                  OMIT COND=(20,10,CH,EQ,C'CHENNAI')

000650 /*

000660 //
```

21. Program to sort given PS in CH mode [reference with two field] and paste the sorted output to another PS without duplicating the records using SORT

```
000100 //TCHN267#       JOB   ABC,NOTIFY=&SYSUID

000200 //STEP1          EXEC  PGM=SORT

000300 //SYSOUT         DD    SYSOUT=*

000400 //SYSPRINT       DD    SYSOUT=*

000500 //SORTIN         DD    DSN=TCHN267.VENKYTSO.PS11,DISP=SHR

000600 //SORTOUT        DD    DSN=TCHN267.VENKYTSO.PS9,DISP=SHR

000620 //SORTWK01       DD    UNIT=SYSDA,SPACE=(CYL,(20,10),RLSE)

000630 //SYSIN          DD    *

000640                  SORT FIELDS=(1,3,CH,D,7,10,CH,A)

000650                  SUM FIELDS=NONE

000660 /*

000670 //
```

22. Program to sort given PS in AC mode and filter by particular word and pass the sorted output to another PS using SORT

```
000100 //TCHN267#       JOB   ABC,NOTIFY=&SYSUID

000200 //STEP1          EXEC  PGM=SORT
```

```
000300 //SYSOUT        DD    SYSOUT=*

000400 //SYSPRINT      DD    SYSOUT=*

000500 //SORTIN        DD    DSN=TCHN267.VENKYTSO.PS11,DISP=SHR

000601 //SORTOF01      DD    DSN=TCHN267.VENKYTSO.PS12,DISP=SHR

000602 //*                  DISP=(NEW,CATLG,DELETE),UNIT=SYSDA,

000603 //*                  SPACE=(CYL,(1,4),RLSE),

000604 //*                  DCB=(RECFM=FB,LRECL=80,BLKSIZE=0)

000605 //SORTOF02      DD    DSN=TCHN267.VENKYTSO.PS13,DISP=SHR

000606 //*                  DISP=(NEW,CATLG,DELETE),UNIT=SYSDA,

000607 //*                  SPACE=(CYL,(1,4),RLSE),

000608 //*                  DCB=(RECFM=FB,LRECL=80,BLKSIZE=0)

000609 //SORTOF03      DD    DSN=TCHN267.VENKYTSO.PS14,DISP=SHR

000610 //*                  DISP=(NEW,CATLG,DELETE),UNIT=SYSDA,

000611 //*                  SPACE=(CYL,(1,4),RLSE),

000612 //*                  DCB=(RECFM=FB,LRECL=80,BLKSIZE=0)

000613 //SORTWK01      DD    UNIT=SYSDA,SPACE=(CYL,(20,10),RLSE)

000620 //SYSIN         DD    *

000630                      SORT FIELDS=COPY

000640           OUTFIL FILES=01,INCLUDE=(20,10,CH,EQ,C'CHENNAI')

000641           OUTFIL FILES=02,INCLUDE=(20,10,CH,EQ,C'MADURAI')

000642           OUTFIL FILES=03,INCLUDE=(20,10,CH,EQ,C'CALCUTTA')

000650 /*

000660 //
```

23. Program to sort given PS in AC mode and filter by particular word and pass the sorted output to non-existing PS using SORT

```
000100 //TCHN267#     JOB   ABC,NOTIFY=&SYSUID

000200 //STEP1        EXEC  PGM=SORT

000300 //SYSOUT       DD    SYSOUT=*

000400 //SYSPRINT     DD    SYSOUT=*

000500 //SORTIN       DD    DSN=TCHN267.VENKYTSO.PS11,DISP=SHR

000600 //SORTOF01     DD    DSN=TCHN267.VENKYTSO.PS15,

000601 //                   DISP=(NEW,CATLG,DELETE),UNIT=SYSDA,

000602 //                   SPACE=(TRK,(1,1),RLSE),

000603 //                   DCB=(RECFM=FB,LRECL=80,BLKSIZE=0)

000604 //SORTOF02     DD    DSN=TCHN267.VENKYTSO.PS16,

000605 //                   DISP=(NEW,CATLG,DELETE),UNIT=SYSDA,

000606 //                   SPACE=(TRK,(1,1),RLSE),

000607 //                   DCB=(RECFM=FB,LRECL=80,BLKSIZE=0)

000608 //SORTOF03     DD    DSN=TCHN267.VENKYTSO.PS17,

000609 //                   DISP=(NEW,CATLG,DELETE),UNIT=SYSDA,

000610 //                   SPACE=(TRK,(1,1),RLSE),

000611 //                   DCB=(RECFM=FB,LRECL=80,BLKSIZE=0)

000612 //SORTWK01     DD    UNIT=SYSDA,SPACE=(CYL,(20,10),RLSE)

000613 //SYSIN        DD    *

000614       SORT FIELDS=COPY

000615       OUTFIL FILES=01,INCLUDE=(20,10,CH,EQ,C'CHENNAI')

000616       OUTFIL FILES=02,INCLUDE=(20,10,CH,EQ,C'MADURAI')

000617       OUTFIL FILES=03,INCLUDE=(20,10,CH,EQ,C'CALCUTTA')
```

```
000618 /*

000619 //
```

24. Program to copy selected content from given PS into another PS with different format using SORT

```
000100 //TCHN267#      JOB   ABC,NOTIFY=&SYSUID

000200 //STEP1         EXEC  PGM=SORT

000300 //SYSOUT        DD    SYSOUT=*

000400 //SYSPRINT      DD    SYSOUT=*

000500 //SORTIN        DD    DSN=TCHN267.VENKYTSO.PS11,DISP=SHR

000600 //SORTOUT       DD    DSN=TCHN267.VENKYTSO.PS9,DISP=SHR

000610 //SORTWK01      DD    UNIT=SYSDA,SPACE=(CYL,(20,10),RLSE)

000620 //SYSIN         DD    *

000630          SORT FIELDS=COPY

000640          INREC FIELDS=(7:1,3,20:7,8)

000650 /*

000660 //
```

25. Program to copy selected content from given PS into another PS with different format using SORT

```
000100 //TCHN267#      JOB   ABC,NOTIFY=&SYSUID

000200 //STEP1         EXEC  PGM=SORT

000300 //SYSOUT        DD    SYSOUT=*

000400 //SYSPRINT      DD    SYSOUT=*

000500 //SORTIN        DD    DSN=TCHN267.VENKYTSO.PS11,DISP=SHR

000600 //SORTOUT       DD    DSN=TCHN267.VENKYTSO.PS9,DISP=SHR
```

```
000610 //SORTWK01    DD    UNIT=SYSDA,SPACE=(CYL,(20,10),RLSE)

000620 //SYSIN       DD    *

000630         SORT FIELDS=COPY

000640         OUTREC FIELDS=(7:1,3,20:7,8)

000650 /*

000660 //
```

26. Program to copy selected content from given PS into another PS using SORT utility and SKIPREC and STOPAFT parameters.

```
000100 //TCHN267#    JOB   ABC,NOTIFY=&SYSUID

000200 //STEP1       EXEC PGM=SORT

000300 //SYSOUT      DD    SYSOUT=*

000400 //SYSPRINT    DD    SYSOUT=*

000500 //SORTIN      DD    DSN=TCHN267.VENKYTSO.PS11,DISP=SHR

000600 //SORTOUT     DD    DSN=TCHN267.VENKYTSO.PS9,DISP=SHR

000700 //SORTWK01    DD    UNIT=SYSDA,SPACE=(CYL,(20,10),RLSE)

000800 //SYSIN       DD    *

000900         SORT FIELDS=COPY,

001000         SKIPREC=3,

001100         STOPAFT=4

001200 /*

001300 //
```

27. Program to copy selected content from given PS into another PS using SORT utility and SKIPREC and ENDREC parameters.

```
000100 //TCHN267#      JOB   ABC,NOTIFY=&SYSUID

000200 //STEP1         EXEC  PGM=SORT

000300 //SYSOUT        DD    SYSOUT=*

000400 //SYSPRINT      DD    SYSOUT=*

000500 //SORTIN        DD    DSN=TCHN267.VENKYTSO.PS11,DISP=SHR

000600 //SORTOF01      DD    DSN=TCHN267.VENKYTSO.PS9,DISP=SHR

000610 //SORTOF02      DD    DSN=TCHN267.VENKYTSO.PS10,DISP=SHR

000700 //SORTWK01      DD    UNIT=SYSDA,SPACE=(CYL,(20,10),RLSE)

000800 //SYSIN         DD    *

000900         SORT FIELDS=COPY

001000         OUTFIL FILES=01,STARTREC=4,ENDREC=6

001100         OUTFIL FILES=02,STARTREC=1,ENDREC=3

001200 /*

001300 //
```

28. Program to merge given two PS using SORT utility and MERGE parameter

```
000100 //TCHN267#      JOB   ABC,NOTIFY=&SYSUID

000200 //STEP1         EXEC  PGM=SORT

000300 //SYSOUT        DD    SYSOUT=*

000400 //SYSPRINT      DD    SYSOUT=*

000500 //SORTIN01      DD    DSN=TCHN267.VENKYTSO.PS18,DISP=SHR

000600 //SORTIN02      DD    DSN=TCHN267.VENKYTSO.PS19,DISP=SHR

000700 //SORTOUT       DD    DSN=TCHN267.VENKYTSO.PS20,DISP=SHR
```

```
000800 //SYSIN          DD    *

000900        MERGE FIELDS=(1,3,CH,A)

001000 /*

001100 //
```

29. Write a JCL program to create a PS file using PROCEDURE

```
000100 //TCHN267#      JOB   ABC,NOTIFY=&SYSUID

000200 //ABC           PROC

000300 //STEP          EXEC  PGM=IEFBR14

000400 //DD1           DD
       DSN=TCHN267.X.Y,DISP=(NEW,CATLG,DELETE),

000500 //              SPACE=(TRK,(1,1),RLSE),

000600 //              DCB=(LRECL=80,BLKSIZE=800,RECFM=FB)

000700 //ABC           PEND

000800 //STEP1         EXEC PROC=ABC
```

30. Program to create a PS file using PROCEDURE

```
000100 //TCHN267#      JOB   ABC,NOTIFY=&SYSUID

000200 //ABC           PROC

000300 //STEP          EXEC  PGM=IEFBR14

000400 //DD1           DD
       DSN=TCHN267.X.Y,DISP=(NEW,CATLG,DELETE),

000500 //              SPACE=(TRK,(1,1),RLSE),

000600 //              DCB=(LRECL=80,BLKSIZE=800,RECFM=FB)

000700 //ABC           PEND

000800 //STEP1         EXEC  PROC=ABC
```

31. Program and procedure to create a PS file

```
000100 //TCHN267#     JOB   ABC,NOTIFY=&SYSUID

000200 //ABC          PROC

000300 //STEP         EXEC  PGM=IEFBR14

000400 //DD1          DD
       DSN=TCHN267.X.Y,DISP=(NEW,CATLG,DELETE),

000500 //             SPACE=(TRK,(1,1),RLSE),

000600 //             DCB=(LRECL=80,BLKSIZE=800,RECFM=FB)

000700 //ABC          PEND

000800 //STEP1        EXEC PROC=ABC
```

32. Program and procedure to create a PS file

Procedure:

```
000200 //IEFBR        PROC

000300 //STEP1        EXEC  PGM=IEFBR14

000400 //DD1          DD    DSN=&A,DISP=(NEW,CATLG,DELETE),

000500 //             SPACE=(TRK,(1,1),RLSE),

000600 //             DCB=(LRECL=80,BLKSIZE=800,RECFM=FB)

000700 //    PEND
```

Program:

```
000100 //TCHN267#     JOB              ABC,NOTIFY=&SYSUID

000200 //JOBPROC      JCLLIB    ORDER=TCHN267.VENKY.JCL

000300 //STEP2        EXEC      IEFBR,A=TCHN267.X.B
```

33. Program and procedure to delete a PS file

Procedure:

```
000100 //PDSDEL1      PROC

000200 //PDSCRTS1     EXEC PGM=IEFBR14

000300 //TEMPLIB1     DD    DISP=(OLD,DELETE),DSN=&DSNAME,

000500 //                   SPACE=(TRK,(1,1),RLSE),

000600 //
     DCB=(RECFM=FB,LRECL=80,BLKSIZE=800,DSORG=PO)

000700 //             PEND
```

Program:

```
000100 //TCHN267#     JOB         ABC,NOTIFY=&SYSUID

000200 //JOBPROC      JCLLIB      ORDER=TCHN267.VENKY.JCL

000300 //STEP2        EXEC
     PDSDEL1,DSNAME=TCHN267.VENKY.JCLTST
```

34. Procedure to create a PS file by overriding already given DSN name.

```
000100 //TCHN267#     JOB   ABC,NOTIFY=&SYSUID

000200 //IEFBR        PROC

000300 //STEP1        EXEC PGM=IEFBR14

000400 //DD1          DD
     DSN=TCHN267.XY.XY,DISP=(NEW,CATLG,DELETE),

000500 //                   SPACE=(TRK,(1,1),RLSE),

000600 //                   DCB=(LRECL=80,BLKSIZE=800,RECFM=FB)

000700 //             PEND

000800 //STEP2        EXEC  IEFBR

000900 //STEP1.DD1    DD    DSN=TCHN267.ZZ.YY
```

35. Procedure and program to delete a PS from DSLIST

Program:

```
000100 //TCHN267#    JOB         ABC,NOTIFY=&SYSUID

000200 //JOBPROC     JCLLIB ORDER=TCHN267.VENKY.JCL

000300 //STEP2       EXEC
       PDSDEL2,DSNAME=TCHN267.VENKYTSO.PS1
```

Procedure:

```
000100 //PDSDEL2     PROC

000200 //PDSCRTS1    EXEC PGM=IEFBR14

000300 //TEMPLIB1    DD      DISP=(OLD,DELETE),DSN=&DSNAME,

000400 //                    SPACE=(TRK,(1,1),RLSE),

000500 //
       DCB=(RECFM=FB,LRECL=80,BLKSIZE=800,DSORG=PS)

000600 //                    PEND
```

36. Procedure and program for copying particular contents from one PS from another PS.

Program:

```
000100 //TCHN267#    JOB         ABC,NOTIFY=&SYSUID

000200 //JOBPROC     JCLLIB   ORDER=TCHN267.VENKY.JCL

000300 //STEP2       EXEC      PDSCPY1,A=TCHN267.VENKYTSO.PS11,

000400 //                      B=TCHN267.VENKYTSO.PS9

000410 //SYSIN       DD        *

000420       SORT FIELDS=COPY

000430       OUTREC FIELDS=(7:1,3,20:7,8)

000440 /*
```

```
000500 //
```

Procedure:

```
000100 //PDSCPY1      PROC
000120 //STEP1        EXEC  PGM=SORT
000130 //SYSOUT       DD    SYSOUT=*
000140 //SYSPRINT     DD    SYSOUT=*
000150 //SORTIN       DD    DSN=&A,DISP=SHR
000160 //SORTOUT      DD    DSN=&B,DISP=SHR
000170 //SORTWK01     DD    UNIT=SYSDA,SPACE=(CYL,(20,10),RLSE)
000193 //      PEND
```

37. Program to create a KSDS VSAM file

```
000100 //TCHN267#     JOB   ABC,NOTIFY=&SYSUID
000200 //STEP         EXEC PGM=IDCAMS
000300 //SYSPRINT     DD    SYSOUT=*
000400 //SYSIN        DD *
000500      DEFINE CLUSTER(NAME(TCHN267.VENKY.KSDS)  -
000600      VOLUMES(TCHN01) -
000700      TRACKS(3,3)  -
000800      RECORDSIZE(80,80) -
000900      KEYS(4,0)  -
001000      INDEXED ) -
001100      DATA(NAME(TCHN267.VENKY.KSDS.DATA)) -
001200      INDEX(NAME(TCHN267.VENKY.KSDS.INDEX) -
001300      )
```

```
001400 /*

001500 //
```

38. Program to create a ESDS VSAM file

```
000100 //TCHN267#      JOB   ABC,NOTIFY=&SYSUID

000200 //STEP          EXEC PGM=IDCAMS

000300 //SYSPRINT      DD    SYSOUT=*

000400 //SYSIN         DD    *

000500      DEFINE CLUSTER(NAME(TCHN267.VENKY.ESDS) -

000600      VOLUMES(TCHN01) -

000700      TRACKS(3,3) -

000800      RECORDSIZE(80,80) -

000900      KEYS(4,0) -

001000      NONINDEXED ) -

001100      DATA(NAME(TCHN267.VENKY.ESDS.DATA)) -

001400 /*

001410 //*   INDEX(NAME(TCHN267.VENKY.KSDS.INDEX) -

001500 //
```

39. Program to create RRDS VSAM file

```
000100 //TCHN267#      JOB   ABC,NOTIFY=&SYSUID

000200 //STEP          EXEC PGM=IDCAMS

000300 //SYSPRINT      DD    SYSOUT=*

000400 //SYSIN         DD    *

000500      DEFINE CLUSTER(NAME(TCHN267.VENKY.RRDS) -

000600      VOLUMES(TCHN01) -
```

```
000700        TRACKS(3,3) -

000800        RECORDSIZE(80,80) -

000900        KEYS(4,0) -

001000        NUMBERED ) -

001100        DATA(NAME(TCHN267.VENKY.RRDS.DATA))

001300 /*

001500 //
```

40. Program to copy the content from a PS file into a KSDS VSAM file

```
000100 //TCHN267#      JOB   ABC,NOTIFY=&SYSUID

000200 //STEP          EXEC PGM=IDCAMS

000300 //SYSPRINT      DD    SYSOUT=*

001200 //DDIN          DD    DSN=TCHN267.VENKYTSO.PS22,DISP=SHR

001300 //DDOUT         DD    DSN=TCHN267.VENKY.KSDS,DISP=OLD

001400 //SYSIN         DD    *

001500        REPRO    -

001600        INFILE(DDIN) -

001700        OUTFILE(DDOUT)

001800 /*

001900 //
```

41. Program to copy the content from a PS file into a KSDS VSAM file

```
000100 //TCHN267#      JOB   ABC,NOTIFY=&SYSUID

000200 //STEP          EXEC PGM=IDCAMS

000300 //SYSPRINT      DD    SYSOUT=*

000600 //SYSIN         DD    *
```

```
000700          REPRO    -

000800             INDATASET(TCHN267.VENKYTSO.PS22)  -

000900             OUTDATASET(TCHN267.VENKY.KSDS1)

001000 /*

001100 //
```

42. Program to print a KSDS VSAM file in SPOOL area in CHAR mode

```
000100 //TCHN267#       JOB    ABC,NOTIFY=&SYSUID

000200 //STEP           EXEC PGM=IDCAMS

000300 //SYSPRINT       DD     SYSOUT=*

000310 //DDIN           DD     DSN=TCHN267.VENKY.KSDS,DISP=SHR

000400 //SYSIN          DD     *

000500          PRINT -

000600          INFILE(DDIN)  -

000700          CHAR

000800 /*

000900 //
```

43. Program to print a KSDS VSAM file in SPOOL area in HEX mode

```
000100 //TCHN267#       JOB    ABC,NOTIFY=&SYSUID

000200 //STEP           EXEC PGM=IDCAMS

000300 //SYSPRINT       DD     SYSOUT=*

000310 //SYSIN          DD     *

000320          PRINT -

000330             INDATASET(TCHN267.VENKY.KSDS)  -

000340          HEX
```

```
000350 /*

000360 //
```

44. Program to print a KSDS VSAM file in SPOOL area in DUMP mode

```
000100 //TCHN267#      JOB   ABC,NOTIFY=&SYSUID

000200 //STEP          EXEC PGM=IDCAMS

000300 //SYSPRINT      DD    SYSOUT=*

000310 //SYSIN         DD    *

000320        PRINT -

000330          INDATASET(TCHN267.VENKY.KSDS) -

000340        DUMP

000350 /*

000360 //
```

45. Program to create an alternate index for a VSAM file

```
000100 //TCHN267#      JOB   ABC,NOTIFY=&SYSUID

000200 //STEP          EXEC PGM=IDCAMS

000300 //SYSPRINT      DD    SYSOUT=*

000301 //BASECLST      DD    DSN=TCHN267.VENKY.KSDS,DISP=SHR

000302 //ALTINDEX      DD    DSN=TCHN267.VENKY.AIX2,DISP=SHR

000310 //SYSIN         DD    *

000320        BLDINDEX INFILE(BASECLST) -

000330          OUTFILE(ALTINDEX)

000350 /*

000360 //
```

46. Program to create an path for an alternate index of VSAM file

```
000100 //TCHN267#      JOB   ABC,NOTIFY=&SYSUID
000200 //STEP          EXEC PGM=IDCAMS
000300 //SYSPRINT      DD    SYSOUT=*
000301 //DD1           DD    DSN=TCHN267.VENKY.KSDS,DISP=SHR
000302 //DD2           DD    DSN=TCHN267.VENKY.AIX2,DISP=SHR
000303 //SYSIN         DD    *
000304       DEFINE PATH(NAME(TCHN267.VENKY.PATH1)  -
000305       PATHENTRY(TCHN267.VENKY.AIX2) -
000306       UPDATE)
000307 /*
000308 //
```

47. Program to copy from one PS to another RRDS with SKIP and COUNT parameter

```
000100 //TCHN267#      JOB   ABC,NOTIFY=&SYSUID
000200 //STEP          EXEC PGM=IDCAMS
000300 //SYSPRINT      DD    SYSOUT=*
000400 //DDIN          DD    DSN=TCHN267.VENKYTSO.PS22,DISP=SHR
000500 //DDOUT         DD    DSN=TCHN267.VENKY.RRDS1,DISP=OLD
000600 //SYSIN         DD    *
000700       REPRO   -
000800       INFILE(DDIN)  -
000900       OUTFILE(DDOUT) -
000910       SKIP(2) -
```

```
000920          COUNT(2)

001000 /*

001100 //
```

48. Program to copy from one PS to another RRDS with SKIP and COUNT parameter

```
000100 //TCHN267#      JOB   ABC,NOTIFY=&SYSUID

000200 //STEP          EXEC PGM=IDCAMS

000300 //SYSPRINT      DD    SYSOUT=*

000400 //DDIN          DD    DSN=TCHN267.VENKYTSO.PS22,DISP=SHR

000500 //DDOUT         DD    DSN=TCHN267.VENKY.ESDS1,DISP=OLD

000600 //SYSIN         DD    *

000700       REPRO    -

000800       INFILE(DDIN)  -

000900       OUTFILE(DDOUT) -

000910       COUNT(2) -

000920       SKIP(2)

000930 /*

000940 //
```

49. Program to copy from one ESDS to another PS with FROMADDRESS and TOADDRESS parameter

```
000100 //TCHN267#      JOB   ABC,NOTIFY=&SYSUID

000200 //STEP          EXEC PGM=IDCAMS

000300 //SYSPRINT      DD    SYSOUT=*

000400 //DDIN          DD    DSN=TCHN267.VENKY.ESDS1,DISP=SHR
```

```
000500 //DDOUT        DD   DSN=TCHN267.VENKYTSO.PS23,DISP=OLD

000600 //SYSIN        DD   *

000700        REPRO   -

000800        INFILE(DDIN)  -

000900        OUTFILE(DDOUT) -

000910        FROMADDRESS(80) -

000920        TOADDRESS(160)

000930 /*

000940 //
```

50. Program to copy from one RRDS to another PS with FROMNUMBER and TONUMBER parameter

```
000100 //TCHN267#     JOB   ABC,NOTIFY=&SYSUID

000200 //STEP         EXEC PGM=IDCAMS

000300 //SYSPRINT     DD   SYSOUT=*

000400 //DDIN         DD   DSN=TCHN267.VENKY.RRDS1,DISP=SHR

000500 //DDOUT        DD   DSN=TCHN267.VENKYTSO.PS24,DISP=OLD

000600 //SYSIN        DD   *

000700        REPRO   -

000800        INFILE(DDIN)  -

000900        OUTFILE(DDOUT) -

000910        FROMNUMBER(1) -

000920        TONUMBER(2)

000930 /*

000940 //
```

51. Program to copy from one KSDS to another PS with FROMNUMBER and TONUMBER parameter

```
000100 //TCHN267#      JOB  ABC,NOTIFY=&SYSUID

000200 //STEP          EXEC PGM=IDCAMS

000300 //SYSPRINT      DD   SYSOUT=*

000400 //DDIN          DD   DSN=TCHN267.VENKY.KSDS1,DISP=SHR

000500 //DDOUT         DD   DSN=TCHN267.VENKYTSO.PS25,DISP=OLD

000600 //SYSIN         DD   *

000700      REPRO    -

000800      INFILE(DDIN)  -

000900      OUTFILE(DDOUT) -

000910      FROMKEY(1002) -

000920      TOKEY(1004)

000930 /*

000940 //
```

52. Program to view the information of a KSDS file in ALL mode using LISTCAT parameter

```
000100 //TCHN267#      JOB  ABC,NOTIFY=&SYSUID

000200 //STEP          EXEC PGM=IDCAMS

000300 //SYSPRINT      DD   SYSOUT=*

000600 //SYSIN         DD   *

000700      LISTCAT ENTRIES(TCHN267.VENKY.KSDS1) ALL

000930 /*

000940 //
```

53. Program to view the information of a KSDS file in NAME mode using LISTCAT parameter

```
000100 //TCHN267#          JOB   ABC,NOTIFY=&SYSUID

000200 //STEP         EXEC PGM=IDCAMS

000300 //SYSPRINT      DD    SYSOUT=*

000600 //SYSIN         DD    *

000700      LISTCAT ENTRIES(TCHN267.VENKY.KSDS1) NAME

000930 /*

000940 //
```

54. Program to view the information of a KSDS file in HISTORY mode using LISTCAT parameter

```
000100 //TCHN267#      JOB   ABC,NOTIFY=&SYSUID

000200 //STEP         EXEC PGM=IDCAMS

000300 //SYSPRINT      DD    SYSOUT=*

000600 //SYSIN         DD    *

000700      LISTCAT ENTRIES(TCHN267.VENKY.KSDS1) HISTORY

000930 /*

000940 //
```

55. Program to view the information of a KSDS file in ALLOCATION mode using LISTCAT parameter

```
000100 //TCHN267#      JOB   ABC,NOTIFY=&SYSUID

000200 //STEP         EXEC PGM=IDCAMS

000300 //SYSPRINT      DD    SYSOUT=*

000600 //SYSIN         DD    *
```

```
000700        LISTCAT ENTRIES(TCHN267.VENKY.KSDS1) ALLOCATION

000930 /*

000940 //
```

56. Program to create a GDG member

```
000100 //TCHN267#      JOB   ABC,NOTIFY=&SYSUID

000200 //STEP          EXEC PGM=IEFBR14

000300 //DD1           DD
        DSN=TCHN267.FILE1.GDG(+1),DISP=(NEW,CATLG,DELETE),

000310 //                 SPACE=(TRK,(1,1),RLSE),

000320 //                 DCB=(LRECL=80,BLKSIZE=800,RECFM=FB)

000330 //
```

57. Program to alter a partitioned data set name using ALTER command

```
000100 //TCHN267#      JOB   ABC,NOTIFY=&SYSUID

000200 //STEP1         EXEC PGM=IDCAMS

000300 //SYSPRINT      DD    SYSOUT=*

000400 //SYSIN         DD    *

000500     ALTER TCHN267.VENKY.PDS1(MEM1)             -

000600     NEWNAME(TCHN267.VENKY.PDS1(MEM2))

000700 /*

000800 //
```

58. Program to write-protect a partitioned data set name using ALTER command

```
000100 //TCHN267#      JOB   ABC,NOTIFY=&SYSUID

000200 //STEP1         EXEC PGM=IDCAMS
```

```
000300 //SYSPRINT     DD     SYSOUT=*

000400 //SYSIN        DD     *

000500     ALTER                              -

000600     TCHN267.VENKY.KSDS.DATA            -

000700      INHIBIT

000800     ALTER                          -

000900     TCHN267.VENKY.KSDS.INDEX       -

001000     INHIBIT

001100 /*

001200 //
```

59. Program to disable write-protected property of KSDS file using ALTER command

```
000100 //TCHN267#     JOB    ABC,NOTIFY=&SYSUID

000200 //STEP1        EXEC PGM=IDCAMS

000300 //SYSPRINT     DD     SYSOUT=*

000400 //SYSIN        DD     *

000500     ALTER                          -

000600     TCHN267.VENKY.KSDS.DATA        -

000700      UNINHIBIT

000800     ALTER                      -

000900     TCHN267.VENKY.KSDS.INDEX       -

001000     UNINHIBIT

001100 /*

001200 //
```

60. Write a JCL program to delete a KSDS file using DELETE command

```
000100 //TCHN267#      JOB   ABC,NOTIFY=&SYSUID

000200 //STEP1         EXEC PGM=IDCAMS

000300 //SYSPRINT      DD    SYSOUT=*

000400 //SYSIN         DD    *

000500      DELETE TCHN267.VENKY.KSDS

000600 /*

000700 //
```

61. Program to delete member of a partitioned dataset using DELETE command

```
000100 //TCHN267#      JOB   ABC,NOTIFY=&SYSUID

000200 //STEP1         EXEC PGM=IDCAMS

000300 //SYSPRINT      DD    SYSOUT=*

000400 //SYSIN         DD    *

000500      DELETE TCHN267.VENKY.PDS1(MEM1)

000600 /*

000700 //
```

JCL & VSAM

Programming Guide

PART - II

Reference Guide

1. JCL Abbreviations

Statement Name	Abbreviations
ALLOCATE	ALC
ASSIGN	ASG
ATTACH	ATT
CATALOG	CAT
CATBUILD	CBD
CATCHECK	CCK
CATDELET	CDL
CATEXTD	CEXT
CATLIST	CLS
CATMAINT	CMN
CATMOVE	CMV
COBOL	CBL
COMMENT	COMM
COMPARE	CMP
CONSOLE	CNSL
CREATE	CR
DEALLOC	DALC
DEFINE	DEF
DMLPROC	DMLP
ENDDATA	EDATA
ENDINPUT	EIN
ENDJOB	EJOB

ENDSTEP	EST ESTP
EXECUTE	EXC
FILCHECK	FCK
FILDUPLI	FDUP
FILMODIF	FMOD
FILREST	FRST
FILSAVE	FSV
FORTRAN77	F7C
INPUT	IN
INVOKE	IVK IV
JASMAINT	MNJAS
LABEL	LBL
LIBALLOC	LALC
LIBDELET	LDL
LIBMAINT	LMN
LINKER	LINK LK
MERGE	MRG
MESSAGE	MSG
MODIFY	MOD
MODVL	MVL
OUTVAL	OVL
PREALLOC	PALC
PREFIX	PFX
PRINT	PR
QASSIGN	QASG

RELEASE	RLS
REPLACE	REPL
REPORT	RPT
SFLIST	SFLS
SHIFT	SHF
SIZE	SZ
SORTFMT	SFMT
SORDIDX	SIDX
SORTWORK	SWK
STEP	STP
SWINPUT	SWI
SYSOUT	SYO
UNCAT	UNC
VALUES	VALUE VL
VOLCHECK	VCK
VOLCOMP	VCMP
VOLDUPPLI	VDUP
VOLPREP	VPRP
VOLREST	VRST
VOLSAVE	VSV
WRITER	WR

2. JCL Error Codes

Error Code	Description
00	Successful completion
02	Duplicate key, Non unique key, Alt index
04	Record length mismatch
05 & 35	Open file not present
10	End of file
14	RRN(Relative record no) > Relative key data
20	Invalid Key VSAM KSDS/RRDS
21	Sequence error on write/ changing key on re-write
22	Duplicate key found
23	Record/file not found
24 & 34 & 44	Boundary violation
30	Data error
37	Open mode not compact with the device
38	Opening file closed with lock
39	Open, file attributes conflicting
41	File is open
42	File is closed
43	Delete/Rewrite & invalid read
46	Sequential read without positioning
47	Reading file not open
48	Write without open IO
91	VSAM password failure

92	Opening an already open file
93	VSAM resource not available
94	VSAM sequential read after end of file
95	VSAM invalid file information
96	VSAM missing DD statement in JCL
97	VSAM open ok, file integrity verified

3. JCL Abend Codes

Abend Code	Description
SB37	Insufficient disk space
SD37	Insufficient disk space
SE37	Insufficient disk space
S80A	Region too small for the program to run
S804	Region too small for the program to run
S822	The requested region is not available
S122	The job was canceled because it violated some restriction. A dump was requested.
S222	The job was cancelled because it violated some restriction. No dump was requested.
S322	The job used more CPU time than it should have. Either the estimate is wrong or the program is in an uncontrolled loop.
S522	Job was waiting too long.
S722	Too many lines of print.
S706	The program on the library was not executable. See linkage editor report that put the program on library.
S806	Program not on the library. May need a JOBLIB or STEPLIB.
S0C1	<ul><li>Executing a program with an unresolved external reference.</li><li>Calling a program and the program was not included during link edit.</li><li>An uncontrolled loop moved data on top of instructions.</li><li>Reading a file that is not open</li><li>SORTIN DCB was not correct</li><li>Mixing compile options RES and NORES in different modules</li></ul>

S0C4	• An uncontrolled loop moved data on top of instructions. • Referencing a field in a record of a closed file • Referencing an item in Linkage-Section when there was no PARM= in the JCL. • Calling/called programs have different length for items passed in Linkage Section with COBOL Sort, doing a STOP RUN or GOBACK while an input or output procedure is still running
S0C5	• See reasons as for 0C4. • Falling through into an ENTRY statement. • Transferring control into the middle of a SORT procedure.
S0C7	• Program attempting to do math on illegal data. • Data is not numeric, but should be. • Moving ZEROS to group item whose subordinate items are packed-decimal • Uninitialized packed-decimal fields. • Record description is wrong. Field starts or ends in the wrong place in the record. • Find record description of creating program.
S0C8	
S0C9	
S0CA	Decimal point overflow error
S0CB	Attempting to divide by 0 and not using ON SIZE ERROR
S0CC	Floating Pointing
S0CD	Exponent overflow and Underflow exceptions
S013	
S878	
S913	
SB14	
S001-4	• Input file record length is not equal to the length stated in the DD or the FD

	• Wrong length record. • IO error, damaged tape, device malfunction. • With disk, reading a dataset that was allocated but never written to. • Writing to input file. • Concatenation of files with different record lengths or record formats.
SOC1-5	• Reading after the end of the file by non-COBOL program. • COBOL intercepts this and displays "QSAM error, status 92". • Out of space on output disk file.

4. VSAM Data Set Types

Data Set	Description
ESDS	Entry Sequence Data Set
KSDS	Key Sequenced Data Set
RRDS	Relative Record Data Set
VRRDS	Variable Length Relative Record Data Set
LDS	Linear Data Set
DATA SET OPEN	An OPEN event against a supported data set type
DATA SET CLOSE	A CLOSE event against a supported data set type
DATA SET UPDATE	An UPDATE event against a supported data set type
DATA SET DELETE	A DELETE event of a supported data set type
DATA SET RENAME	A RENAME event of a supported data set type
DATA SET CREATE	A DEFINE or New Allocation event of a supported data set type
DATA SET ALTER	An ALTER of the attributes of a supported data set type
RACF® ALTER	A security facility ALTER access of a supported data set type
RACF CONTROL	A security facility CONTROL access of a supported data set type
RACF UPDATE	A security facility UPDATE access of a supported data set type
RACF READ	A security facility READ access of a supported data set type
KSDS	Key-sequenced data set
RRDS	Relative record data set
VRRDS	Variable length relative record data sets

RECORD INSERT	A record insert within a data set of a supported type.
RECORD DELETE	A record delete within a data set of a supported type.
RECORD READ	A record read within a data set of a supported type.
RECORD UPDATE	A record update within a data set of a supported type.

5. VSAM Error Codes

VSAM EXTENDED RETURN CODE:

Error Code	Description
0	Successful completion
4	Another request is active
8	There is a logical error
12	There is a physical error

VSAM EXTENDED FUNCTION CODE:

Error Code	Description
0	Accessing base cluster, no problem
1	Accessing base cluster, may be a problem
2	Accessing alternate index, no problem
3	Accessing alternate index, may be a problem
4	Upgrade processing, no problem
5	Upgrade processing, may be a problem

VSAM EXTENDED FEEDBACK CODE:

Error Code	Description
4	Read error on data
8	Read error on index
12	Read error in sequence set
16	Write error on data

20	Write error on index
24	Write error in sequence set

VSAM EXTENDED FEEDBACK CODE:

PHYSICAL ERROR:

Error Code	Description
4	Read error on data
8	Read error on index
12	Read error in sequence set
16	Write error on data
20	Write error on index
24	Write error in sequence set

LOGICAL ERROR:

Error Code	Description
4	Read past end of file
8	Duplicate key
12	Key sequence error
16	Not found
20	Control interval in use by other job
24	Volume cannot be mounted
28	Unable to extend dataset
32	RBA not found
36	Key is not in a defined key range
40	Insufficient virtual storage

64	No available strings
68	Open did not specify proc type
72	Key access to ESDS or RRDS
76	Attempted insert to wrong type dataset
80	Attempted delete from ESDS
84	Optcd loc for put request
88	Position not established
92	Put without get for update
96	Trying to change primary key
100	Trying to change LRECL
104	Invalid RPL options
108	Invalid LRECL
112	Invalid key length
116	Violated load mode restriction
120	Wrong task submitting request
132	Trying to get spanned rec in loc mode
136	Trying to get spanned rec by address
140	Inconsistent spanned rec
144	Alt index pointer with no matching
148	Exceeded max pointers in alt index rec
152	Insufficient buffers available
156	Invalid control interval
192	Invalid relative rec number
196	Attempted addressed request to RRDS
200	Invalid access through a path

204	Put in backward mode
208	Invalid ENDREQ macro
252	Record mode processing is not allowed for a Linear data set